DISCARD

Drinks on the Lanai

Drinks on the Lanai

COCKTAILS, MOCKTAILS & CHEESECAKE

INSPIRED BY
THE GOLDEN GIRLS

Elouise Anders

WITH ILLUSTRATIONS BY
Mel Baxter

Smith Street Books

Contents

INTRODUCTION

6

TALL and SASSY

9

FUN and FLIRTY

43

BASICS

144

DRINKING *all* **DAY**

111

SHORT *and* **BOOZY**

77

DRINK INDEX

150

Introduction

With age comes wisdom. With wisdom comes retirement. And, if you're lucky, retirement might even come with a lanai. Pronounced 'lan-eye', this style of open-sided patio has long been an architectural standard in Hawaii. Throughout the mid-20th century, as Hawaii became emblematic of rest and relaxation, the lanai made its way to the mainland. In Miami, Florida, they're considered a beach-chic staple. And, as any fans of the show will know, there is a glorious lanai attached to the house in TV's *The Golden Girls*.

Dorothy Zbornak, Blanche Devereaux, Sophia Petrillo and Rose Nylund first blessed our TV screens in 1985, and *The Golden Girls* was an instant success. Their weekly hijinks ran for seven seasons, as the world watched these four mature-age roommates navigate themes like dating and divorce, friendships new and old, ageing and trying to make ends meet. It was a situation comedy unlike anything we'd ever seen, and even now, decades later in the age of streaming, the show maintains a cult status. There's no doubt that – just like its four leading ladies – *The Golden Girls* only gets better with age.

Throughout the series, these four girls always loved a cocktail. And what better place to tipple than out on their shared lanai, while watching a Miami sunset? In this book, Dorothy, Blanche, Sophia and Rose each have a chapter to share recipes for their favourite tropical cocktails. From the classic Piña Colada (page 44), to the incredibly boozy Pineapple Negroni (page 79), there's something for everyone and for every occasion. (Lanai or no.)

To shake, stir, strain and generally ready these cocktails, make sure you've got the right equipment. Any standard cocktail shaker set should suffice for most recipes in this book, but a quality high-speed blender would go a long way to ensuring your frozen margaritas are always *muy bueno*. In terms of glassware, you can get as creative as you like. If you don't have a dedicated highball glass, just use anything tall. No old fashioned glass? Any old short tumbler will suffice. As you'll see, some of the wilder recipes in this book, such as the Coconut Rum (page 122), suggest an entire coconut as the ideal drinking vessel. But all you really need for a successful cocktail hour is an old mug and a good attitude.

1

TALL *and* SASSY

After 38 years married to Stan, wouldn't you need a drink? Dorothy Zbornak does. She prefers a tall glass, as they are best for brandishing wildly to prove a point.

MARA AMU

SERVES 1

3 teaspoons white rum

3 teaspoons gold rum

3 teaspoons dark rum

20 ml (¾ fl oz) freshly squeezed lime juice

20 ml (¾ fl oz) freshly squeezed orange juice

20 ml (¾ fl oz) freshly squeezed grapefruit juice

20 ml (¾ fl oz) Passionfruit syrup (page 147)

pink grapefruit wedge, for garnish

Place all the ingredients (except the garnish) in a high-speed blender with 1 cup crushed ice.

Blend at high speed for 5 seconds.

Pour into a Mara Amu mug or tall glass. Garnish with a pink **grapefruit** wedge.

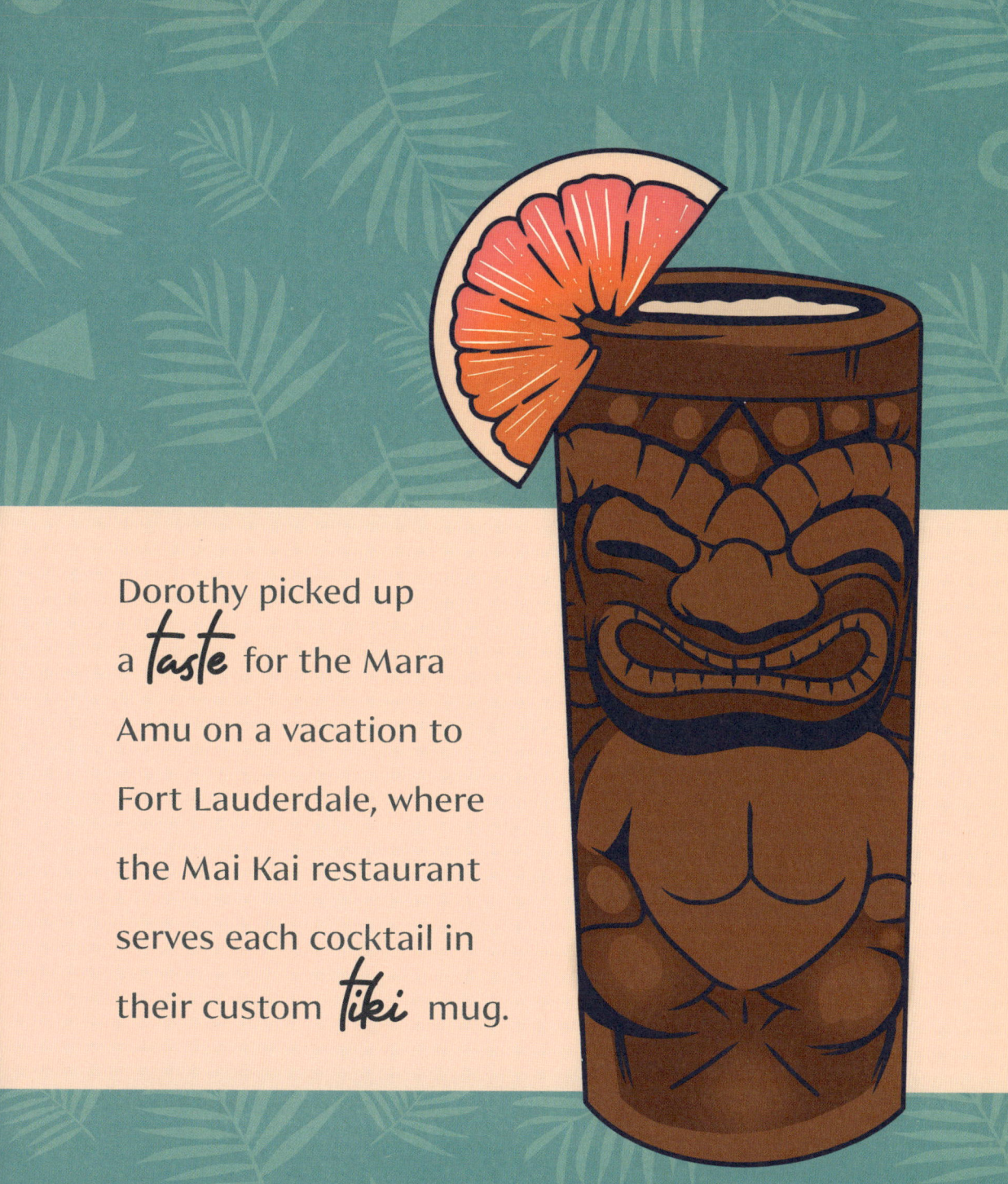

Dorothy picked up a *taste* for the Mara Amu on a vacation to Fort Lauderdale, where the Mai Kai restaurant serves each cocktail in their custom *tiki* mug.

This cocktail blends *two rums* together, with a third floating on top. What more do you need to know?

RUM RUNNER

SERVES 1

30 ml (1 fl oz) dark rum

30 ml (1 fl oz) white rum

30 ml (1 fl oz) blackberry liqueur

30 ml (1 fl oz) banana liqueur

30 ml (1 fl oz) freshly squeezed orange juice

30 ml (1 fl oz) pineapple juice, fresh if possible

2 teaspoons grenadine

3 teaspoons 151 proof white rum (optional)

orange peel, for garnish

Place the dark and white rums, liqueurs and fruit juices in a high-speed blender with 1 cup crushed ice. Blend until smooth.

Pour into a hurricane glass and add the grenadine. If using, float the 151 proof rum on top by pouring it over the back of a spoon.

Garnish with an orange peel.

PI YI

SERVES 1

30 ml (1 fl oz) white rum

30 ml (1 fl oz) gold rum

45 ml (1½ fl oz) pineapple juice, fresh if possible

3 teaspoons Honey syrup (page 148)

3 teaspoons Passionfruit syrup (page 147)

1 dash orange bitters

hollowed pineapple, for serving (optional)

pineapple leaves, maraschino cherries and lime wheel, for garnish

Place the rums, pineapple juice, syrups and bitters in a high-speed blender with ½ cup crushed ice. Blend at high speed for 5 seconds.

Pour into a hollowed-out pineapple (or large cocktail glass) and top with crushed ice.

Garnish with pineapple leaves, maraschino cherries and lime wheel.

A more *lanai*-appropriate drink is hard to find, as the Pi Yi is the international symbol of 'Can't you see I'm busy *relaxing*?'

HURRICANE

Anyone who's been to *New Orleans* has tried one of these insane concoctions. Not for the faint of heart *(or liver)*.

SERVES 1

- 60 ml (2 fl oz/¼ cup) white rum
- 60 ml (2 fl oz/¼ cup) dark rum
- 30 ml (1 fl oz) freshly squeezed lime juice
- 30 ml (1 fl oz) freshly squeezed orange juice
- 60 ml (2 fl oz/¼ cup) passionfruit pulp
- 3 teaspoons Passionfruit syrup (page 147)
- 3 teaspoons sugar syrup
- 3 teaspoons grenadine
- 1 teaspoon Orgeat syrup (page 149)
- orange wheel and maraschino cherry, for garnish

Combine the ingredients (except the garnish) in a cocktail shaker with ice. Shake.

Strain into a hurricane glass filled with ice. Garnish with an orange wheel and maraschino cherry.

BAHAMA MAMA

A *tropical* getaway in a glass (that's also filled with plenty of rum).

SERVES 1

30 ml (1 fl oz) dark rum

3 teaspoons white rum

3 teaspoons coconut rum

90 ml (3 fl oz) pineapple juice, fresh if possible

60 ml (2 fl oz/¼ cup) freshly squeezed orange juice

30 ml (1 fl oz) freshly squeezed lemon juice

1 dash orange bitters

1 teaspoon grenadine

3 teaspoons 151 proof rum

pineapple wedge, orange wheel and maraschino cherry, for garnish

Combine the dark, white and coconut rums with the fruit juices and bitters in a cocktail shaker filled with ice. Shake.

Strain into a poco grande or other tall glass filled with ice.

Add the grenadine, pouring it slowly against the inside of the glass (it should sink to the bottom). Float the 151 proof rum on top by pouring it over the back of a spoon.

Garnish with a pineapple wedge, orange wheel and maraschino cherry, and drink through a straw.

TANGAROA

Almond liqueur and mango, an unlikely but *brilliant* combination for a cocktail.

SERVES 1

30 ml (1 fl oz) white rum

30 ml (1 fl oz) gold rum

1½ teaspoons amaretto

60 ml (2 fl oz/¼ cup) mango nectar

3 teaspoons freshly squeezed lime juice

cinnamon stick, for garnish

Combine the ingredients (except the garnish) in a cocktail shaker filled with ice. Shake.

Strain into a chilled champagne flute and garnish with a cinnamon stick.

QUEEN'S ROAD COCKTAIL

SERVES 1

45 ml (1½ fl oz) gold rum

1 teaspoon ginger liqueur

3 teaspoons freshly squeezed lime juice

3 teaspoons freshly squeezed orange juice

3 teaspoons Honey syrup (page 148)

1 dash orange bitters

orange twist, for garnish

Combine the ingredients (except the garnish) in a cocktail shaker filled with ice. Shake.

Strain into a chilled cocktail glass. Garnish with an orange twist.

Ginger liqueur is an underappreciated drop. It adds a spiciness and mouthfeel that can kick your drink up a notch.

This **bright green** and creamy cocktail will get you in the mood for a tropical getaway. Or at the very least to put your feet up and **have another**.

COCO LOCO PINE-LIME

SERVES 1

30 ml (1 fl oz) vodka

30 ml (1 fl oz) coconut rum

30 ml (1 fl oz) melon liqueur

90 ml (3 fl oz) pineapple juice, fresh if possible

30 ml (1 fl oz) cream

pineapple wedge, for garnish

Combine the vodka, rum and liqueur in a poco grande glass filled with crushed ice. Top with pineapple juice, ensuring there's some room left at the top.

Float the cream on top by pouring it over the back of a spoon.

Garnish with a pineapple wedge.

STAN'S MAI TAI

SERVES 1

60 ml (2 fl oz/¼ cup) aged rum

20 ml (¾ fl oz) orange curaçao

20 ml (¾ fl oz) Orgeat syrup (page 149)

20 ml (¾ fl oz) freshly squeezed lime juice

pineapple wedge, lime wedge and maraschino cherry, for garnish

Combine the ingredients (except the garnish) in a cocktail shaker with ice. Shake.

Strain into an old fashioned glass filled with crushed ice. Garnish with pineapple wedge, lime wedge and maraschino cherry.

Stan's favourite tropical beverage is Don the Beachcomber's iconic Mai Tai. One sip and you can almost *feel the sand* between your toes.

'An aphrodisiac? Use *vodka* and *black underwear* like everyone else.'

BEACH-COMBING BRIDE

SERVES 1

60 ml (2 fl oz/¼ cup) white rum

20 ml (¾ fl oz) orange curaçao

20 ml (¾ fl oz) freshly squeezed lime juice

1½ teaspoons maraschino cherry liqueur (or juice)

¼ teaspoon sugar syrup

lime wheel and maraschino cherry, for garnish

Combine the ingredients (except the garnish) in a cocktail shaker filled with ice. Shake.

Strain into a chilled martini glass and garnish with a lime wheel and a maraschino cherry.

PASSIONFRUIT MARG

SERVES 1

45 ml (1½ fl oz) tequila

3 teaspoons Cointreau

pulp from 1 passionfruit (reserve ½ shell)

30 ml (1 fl oz) freshly squeezed lime juice

3 teaspoons Passionfruit syrup (page 147)

salt, for garnish

Combine the tequila, Cointreau, passionfruit pulp, lime juice and passionfruit syrup in a cocktail shaker filled with ice. Shake.

Strain into a large cocktail glass, rimmed with salt.

Place the reserved passionfruit shell on top of the drink, for garnish.

A *twist* on the classic *margarita*, this sweet passionfruit version always needs a salty rim for balance.

Lit ON ARRIVAL

SERVES 1

45 ml (1½ fl oz) gold rum

45 ml (1½ fl oz) dark rum

30 ml (1 fl oz) 151 proof demerara rum

20 ml (¾ fl oz) freshly squeezed lime juice

3 teaspoons Velvet falernum (page 146)

1 teaspoon grenadine

1 teaspoon Pernod

3 teaspoons Don's mix (page 144)

mint sprig, orange wedge, pineapple wedge and maraschino cherries, for garnish

Place the ingredients (except the garnish) in a high-speed blender with ¾ cup crushed ice.

Blend at high speed for 5 seconds.

Pour into a tall tiki glass and top up with ice cubes. Garnish with mint, orange wedge, pineapple wedge and maraschino cherries. And drink responsibly.

CUBA LIBRE

Every bartender worth their weight in limes should be able make this jazzy rum and cola *blindfolded*.

SERVES 1

45 ml (1½ fl oz) dark Cuban rum

30 ml (1 fl oz) freshly squeezed lime juice

60 ml (2 fl oz/¼ cup) cola

lime wedge, for garnish

Combine the ingredients (except the garnish) in a tall glass filled with crushed ice and stir to combine.

Garnish with a lime wedge.

BITTER MAI TAI

SERVES 1

30 ml (1 fl oz) dark rum

45 ml (1½ fl oz) Campari

3 teaspoons orange curaçao

30 ml (1 fl oz) freshly squeezed lime juice

20 ml (¾ fl oz) Orgeat syrup (page 149)

mint sprig, for garnish

Combine the ingredients (except the garnish) in a cocktail shaker filled with ice. Shake.

Strain into an old fashioned glass filled with crushed ice. Garnish with mint.

Campari is the ultimate aperitif, and makes this Mai Tai far more bitter than any of its other variations.

FEDERALI

Although Federali might be a *Spanglish* word, this cocktail is best when made with genuine Mexican agave.

SERVES 1

30 ml (1 fl oz) white rum

30 ml (1 fl oz) aged rum

2 teaspoons agave syrup

2 teaspoons Orgeat syrup (page 149)

30 ml (1 fl oz) freshly squeezed lemon juice

orange wheel, for garnish

Combine the ingredients (except the garnish) in a cocktail shaker filled with ice. Shake.

Strain into an old fashioned glass filled with crushed ice. Garnish with an orange wheel.

DARK and STORMY

SERVES 1

45 ml (1½ fl oz) dark rum

30 ml (1 fl oz) freshly squeezed lime juice

2 dashes orange bitters

60 ml (2 fl oz/¼ cup) ginger beer

lime wedge, for garnish

Combine the ingredients (except the garnish) in a tall glass filled with crushed ice and stir to combine.

Garnish with a lime wedge.

> You can't beat the classic cocktails, and the *dark* and *stormy* is as old as time itself.

APPLE PIE

SERVES 1

- 30 ml (1 fl oz) white rum
- 30 ml (1 fl oz) gold rum
- 3 teaspoons freshly squeezed lime juice
- 3 teaspoons Cinnamon syrup (page 147)
- 60 ml (2 fl oz/¼ cup) cloudy apple juice
- apple slices and ground cinnamon, for garnish

Combine the ingredients (except the garnish) in a cocktail shaker filled with ice. Shake.

Strain into a highball glass filled with ice. Garnish with apple slices and a dusting of cinnamon.

This **cinnamon-y** cocktail is as sweet as apple pie. But it's got **booze** in it, making it superior to its crusted cousin in every way!

This cocktail should be *blindingly* bright. Try and think of the thickest *blue eyeshadow* you've ever seen, and you're halfway there.

BLUE NEON

SERVES 1

60 ml (2 fl oz/¼ cup) vodka

3 teaspoons blue curaçao

100 ml (3½ fl oz) lemonade

maraschino cherry, for garnish

Combine the vodka and curaçao in a tall glass filled with ice. Top with lemonade.

Garnish with a maraschino cherry.

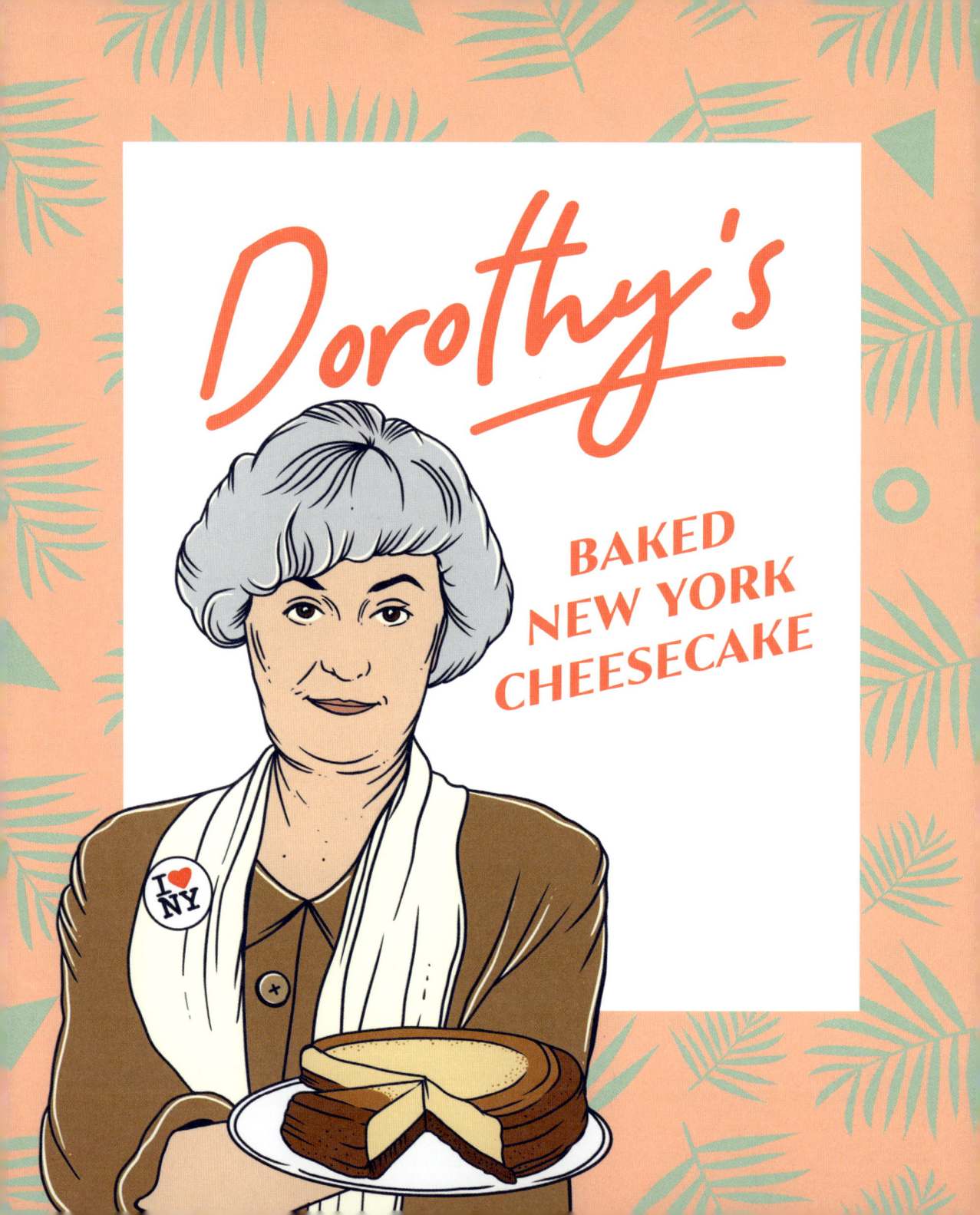

New York City born and raised, Dorothy knows the Manhattan slice still reigns supreme.

SERVES 8

250 g (8½ oz) digestive biscuits (Graham crackers), crushed

125 g (4½ oz) unsalted butter, melted

3½ teaspoons natural vanilla extract

750 g (26 oz) cream cheese, softened

110 g (4 oz) caster (superfine) sugar

1 lemon, zested and juiced

250 g (9 oz) plain (all-purpose) flour

3 large eggs

250 g (8½ oz) sour cream

Preheat the oven to 160°C (320°F) and line a 23 cm (9 in) springform cake tin with baking paper.

Combine the biscuits, butter and ½ teaspoon of vanilla extract until mixed thoroughly. Press evenly into the base of the cake tin. Put in the fridge to chill.

In a large bowl, beat the cream cheese, sugar, remaining 3 teaspoons of vanilla extract, lemon zest and juice until smooth. Sift in the flour and mix until combined. Add the eggs one at a time, beating for 15 seconds after each. Fold in the sour cream until smooth.

Remove the tin from the fridge and pour in the cheesecake mixture. Place in the middle of the oven and bake for 75–90 minutes, or until the cheesecake filling just jiggles with a shake. Turn the oven off and allow the cheesecake to cool completely in the oven (2–3 hours).

Chill overnight before cutting into slices and serving.

2

FUN *and* FLIRTY

Blanche Devereaux might come across as a delicate southern belle, sure. But that doesn't mean she can't knock back a helluva strong cocktail. Or ten.

PIÑA COLADA

SERVES 1

30 ml (1 fl oz) gold rum

30 ml (1 fl oz) white rum

50 ml (1¾ fl oz) coconut milk

40 ml (1¼ fl oz) sugar syrup

80 ml (2½ fl oz/⅓ cup) pineapple juice, fresh if possible

20 ml (¾ fl oz) freshly squeezed lime juice

3 teaspoons double (heavy) cream

pineapple wedge, pineapple leaf and maraschino cherry, for garnish

Place the ingredients (except the garnish) in a high-speed blender with 1 cup ice. Pulse until the ice is crushed.

Pour into a poco grande or other tall glass and garnish with a pineapple wedge, pineapple leaf and maraschino cherry.

Everyone talks about getting caught in the rain when drinking this iconic cocktail. But what about just getting caught up in a three-day bender? Just as likely.

This hard working cocktail is *refreshing*, but still gets the job done.

SAILOR on LEAVE

SERVES 1

30 ml (1 fl oz) dark rum

30 ml (1 fl oz) demerara rum

30 ml (1 fl oz) white rum

20 ml (¾ fl oz) freshly squeezed lime juice

20 ml (¾ fl oz) freshly squeezed grapefruit juice

30 ml (1 fl oz) Honey syrup (page 148)

30 ml (1 fl oz) soda water (seltzer)

orange wheel, orange peel and mint sprig, for garnish

Combine the rums, fruit juices and honey syrup in a cocktail shaker filled with ice. Shake.

Strain into an old fashioned glass filled with crushed ice. Top with the soda water and garnish with an orange wheel, orange peel and mint.

Traditionally this drink is garnished with a frozen 'snow cone' with a straw through the middle. You can make your own by filling a cone-shaped glass with finely crushed ice, poking a straw through the centre and freezing it for a few hours.

CLASSIC DAIQUIRI

A staple cocktail for any afternoon on the lanai. This drink shouts to the world 'It's 5 o'clock *somewhere!*'

SERVES 1

- 60 ml (2 fl oz/¼ cup) white rum
- 30 ml (1 fl oz) freshly squeezed lime juice
- 3 teaspoons sugar syrup
- lime wheel, for garnish

Combine the ingredients (except the garnish) in a cocktail shaker filled with ice. Shake.

Strain into a chilled cocktail glass and garnish with a lime wheel.

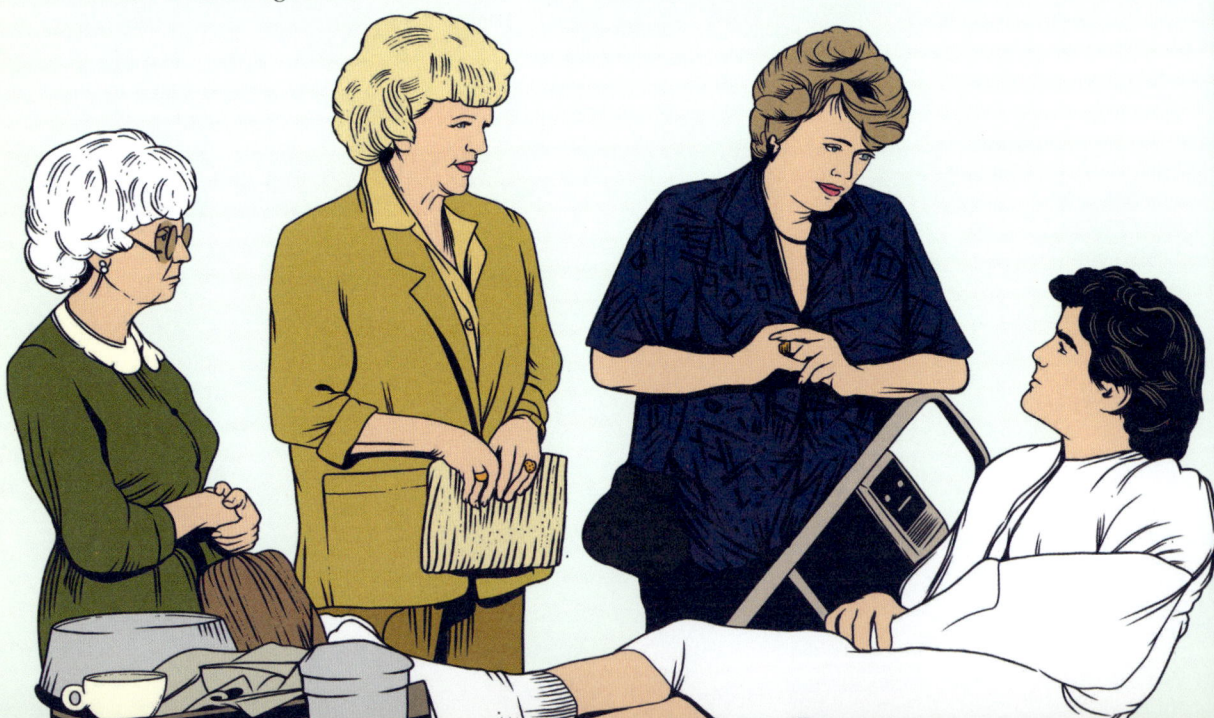

PINEAPPLE DAIQUIRI

SERVES 1

80 g (2¾ oz/½ cup) chopped fresh pineapple

5 mint leaves

60 ml (2 fl oz/¼ cup) pineapple rum

30 ml (1 fl oz) freshly squeezed lime juice

3 teaspoons sugar syrup

pineapple wedge, for garnish

Muddle the pineapple and mint in a cocktail shaker. Add the rum, lime juice and sugar syrup and fill the shaker with ice. Shake vigorously.

Strain into a chilled cocktail glass. Garnish with a pineapple wedge.

A tropical twist on the classic daiquiri, for fans of pineapple and fans of all things good in the world.

FROZEN LIME DAIQUIRI

SERVES 1

90 ml (3 fl oz) white rum

60 ml (2 fl oz/¼ cup) freshly squeezed lime juice

30 ml (1 fl oz) sugar syrup

lime wheel, for garnish

Place the ingredients (except the garnish) in a high-speed blender with 1 cup ice. Blend at high speed until smooth.

Pour into a large cocktail glass and garnish with a lime wheel.

The *best thing* is about frozen cocktails is that you can double or triple the portions easily, for two serves or three serves. All for your own refreshment, of course.

MANGO DAIQUIRI

SERVES 1

1 mango, cheeks removed and stone discarded

60 ml (2 fl oz/¼ cup) white rum

20 ml (¾ fl oz) mango liqueur (optional)

30 ml (1 fl oz) freshly squeezed lime juice

20 ml (¾ fl oz) sugar syrup

lime wheel, for garnish

Scoop the flesh from the mango cheeks and place in a high-speed blender with the rest of the ingredients (except the garnish) and ½ cup crushed ice. Blend at high speed until smooth.

Pour into a large cocktail glass and garnish with a lime wedge.

Although at its most divine and silky when using fresh mangoes, this daiquiri can be made using tinned mangoes in a seasonal pinch.

STRAWBERRY DAIQUIRI

SERVES 1

250 g (9 oz) fresh strawberries, hulled and cut in half

55 g (2 oz/¼ cup) caster (superfine) sugar

30 ml (1 fl oz) freshly squeezed lemon juice

60 ml (2 fl oz/¼ cup) white rum

20 ml (¾ fl oz) strawberry liqueur (optional)

20 ml (¾ fl oz) freshly squeezed lime juice

20 ml (¾ fl oz) sugar syrup

lime wheel and sliced strawberries, for garnish

In a small bowl, combine the strawberries with the sugar and lemon juice. Cover and refrigerate for 30 minutes.

Place the strawberries in a high-speed blender with the rest of the ingredients (except the garnish) and 1 cup ice. Blend at high speed until smooth.

Pour into a large cocktail glass and garnish with a lime wheel and sliced strawberries.

Fresh and *bright* berries are crucial to this *divine daiquiri*, so when strawberries are in season you best get blending.

For this cocktail, if you don't have the specific pearl diver glass (in all its ribbed glory) just use an *open coconut* instead.

MAMA'S PEARLS

SERVES 1

45 ml (1½ fl oz) white rum

3 teaspoons demerara rum

3 teaspoons dark rum

1 tablespoon Velvet falernum (page 146)

30 ml (1 fl oz) freshly squeezed orange juice

20 ml (¾ fl oz) Pearl diver's mix (page 144)

pearl diver glass or opened coconut, for serving (optional)

edible flower and banana leaf, for garnish

Place the ingredients (except the garnish) in a high-speed blender with 1 cup crushed ice. Blend at high speed until smooth.

Pour into a pearl diver glass or coconut and garnish with an edible flower and banana leaf.

'Like I'm the *only* person who's ever mixed a margarita in a sailor's mouth!'

151 SWIZZLE

SERVES 1

45 ml (1½ fl oz) 151 proof demerara rum

3 teaspoons freshly squeezed lime juice

3 teaspoons Don's mix (page 144)

1 dash orange bitters

1 teaspoon Pernod

cinnamon stick, lime wheel and freshly grated nutmeg, for garnish

Place the ingredients (except the garnish) in a high-speed blender with 1 cup crushed ice. Blend at high speed for 5 seconds.

Pour into a chilled swizzle or other stainless steel cup and top up with crushed ice. Garnish with a cinnamon stick, lime wheel and grated nutmeg.

A swizzle is a sour cocktail with Caribbean heritage, but if you can't find one of these traditional stainless steel numbers, then any old highball glass will do.

Named after Trinidad's Queen's Park Hotel, where it was born, this swizzle will **get you sizzling**.

QUEEN'S PARK SWIZ

SERVES 1

3 teaspoons freshly squeezed lime juice

2 sprigs mint, plus extra to garnish

60 ml (2 fl oz/¼ cup) dark rum

2 dashes orange bitters

3 teaspoons sugar syrup

60 ml (2 fl oz/¼ cup) soda water (seltzer)

Place the lime juice and mint in a highball glass. Fill with crushed ice.

Add the rum, bitters and sugar syrup. Stir to combine and top with soda water. Garnish with extra mint.

FROZEN MARG

SERVES 1

60 ml (2 fl oz/¼ cup) tequila

3 teaspoons Cointreau

20 ml (¾ fl oz) freshly squeezed lime juice

20 ml (¾ fl oz) freshly squeezed lemon juice

3 teaspoons sugar syrup

salt and lime wheel, for garnish

Place the ingredients (except the garnish) in a high-speed blender with 1 cup ice. Blend at high speed until smooth.

Pour into a chilled cocktail glass rimmed with salt.

Garnish with a lime wheel.

It's a *classic* for a reason, people! You should always have margarita fixings stashed away for an *impromptu marg*.

JET PILOT

Some people are just *born to fly*. Others, like us, are born to drink cocktails in the back row of the plane. No complaints!

SERVES 1

30 ml (1 fl oz) dark rum

20 ml (¾ fl oz) white rum

20 ml (¾ fl oz) 151 proof demerara rum

1 teaspoon Pernod

3 teaspoons freshly squeezed grapefruit juice

3 teaspoons freshly squeezed lime juice

3 teaspoons Cinnamon syrup (page 147)

1 dash orange bitters

maraschino cherry, for garnish

Place the ingredients (except the garnish) in a high-speed blender with 1 cup ice. Blend at high speed until smooth.

Pour into a large cocktail glass and garnish with a maraschino cherry.

TEST PILOT

SERVES 1

45 ml (1½ fl oz) dark rum

20 ml (¾ fl oz) white rum

2 teaspoons orange curaçao

1 teaspoon Pernod

3 teaspoons freshly squeezed lime juice

3 teaspoons Velvet falernum (page 146)

1 dash orange bitters

orange wheel, for garnish

Place the ingredients (except the garnish) in a high-speed blender with 1 cup ice. Blend at high speed until smooth.

Pour into a large cocktail glass and garnish with an orange wheel.

Someone has to do the valiant job of testing out a cocktail as it's being developed. It's dangerous but rewarding work.

RUM JULEP

This *herb-a-licious* julep is a quirky twist on the classic mint cocktail.

SERVES 1

45 ml (1½ fl oz) demerara rum

3 teaspoons aged rum

3 teaspoons freshly squeezed lime juice

3 teaspoons freshly squeezed orange juice

3 teaspoons Honey syrup (page 148)

¼ teaspoon grenadine

¼ teaspoon Velvet falernum (page 146)

¼ teaspoon Allspice dram (page 145)

1 dash orange bitters

Place the ingredients in a high-speed blender with ½ cup crushed ice. Blend at high speed for 5 seconds.

Pour into a metal julep cup or tall glass and top with crushed ice.

MONTEGO BAY

SERVES 1

20 ml (¾ fl oz) dark rum

20 ml (¾ fl oz) gold rum

20 ml (¾ fl oz) aged rum

1 teaspoon absinthe

3 teaspoons freshly squeezed lime juice

3 teaspoons freshly squeezed grapefruit juice

20 ml (¾ fl oz) Honey syrup (page 148)

1 teaspoon Allspice dram (page 145)

1 dash orange bitters

grapefruit wheel, for garnish

Combine the ingredients (except the garnish) in a cocktail shaker filled with ice. Shake.

Strain into a chilled cocktail glass filled with crushed ice. Garnish with a grapefruit wheel.

A kaleidoscope of rums make the Montego a *formidable* cocktail. You've been warned.

MOJITO

After eons of cocktail drinking, through all the fads and phases, the mojito remains in *mint condition*.

SERVES 1

½ lime, cut into 6 pieces

1 small handful mint leaves

3 teaspoons sugar

60 ml (2 fl oz/¼ cup) dark Cuban rum

45 ml (1½ fl oz) soda water (seltzer).

mint sprig and lime wedge, for garnish

Muddle the lime, mint and sugar in a cocktail shaker. Add the rum and fill the shaker with ice. Shake vigorously.

Pour the contents of the shaker into a tall glass and top with the soda water. Garnish with mint and a lime wedge.

PINEAPPLE MOJITO

SERVES 1

1 lime, cut into 12 pieces

160 g (5½ oz/1 cup) chopped fresh pineapple

1 small handful basil leaves

90 ml (3 fl oz) white rum

30 ml (1 fl oz) sugar syrup

60 ml (2 fl oz/¼ cup) soda water (seltzer)

hollowed-out pineapple, for serving (optional)

lemongrass stalk, for garnish

Muddle the lime, pineapple and basil in a cocktail shaker. Add the rum and sugar syrup, and fill the shaker with crushed ice. Shake vigorously.

Pour the contents of the shaker into a hollowed-out pineapple (or a very large glass) and top up with crushed ice and the soda water. Garnish with lemongrass and two straws.

A twist on the classic Cuban cocktail, that is *dangerously* easy to drink.

What's better than watching a *sunrise* from the lanai? Watching it with this *cocktail in hand*, of course.

TEQUILA SUNRISE

SERVES 1

60 ml (2 fl oz/¼ cup) tequila

90 ml (3 fl oz) freshly squeezed orange juice

3 teaspoons grenadine

orange wedge and maraschino cherry, for garnish

Combine the tequila and orange juice in a tall glass filled with ice.

Slowly add the grenadine, pouring against the inside of the glass so that it sinks to the bottom.

Garnish with an orange wedge and maraschino cherry, and continue on your rock and roll tour.

SALTY SAILOR

SERVES 1

30 ml (1 fl oz) tequila

3 teaspoons Campari

60 ml (2 fl oz/¼ cup) freshly squeezed pink grapefruit juice

salt and pink grapefruit slice, for garnish

Combine the ingredients (except the garnish) in an old fashioned glass rimmed with salt and filled with ice.

Garnish with a pink grapefruit slice.

This grapefruit-y cocktail is the **perfect cure** for sea sickness. (*Disclaimer:* this theory has not been adequately tested.)

The stately manor where Blanche grew up was in Atlanta, Georgia. AKA – peach country!

SERVES 8

250 g (8½ oz) digestive biscuits (Graham crackers), crushed

15 g (½ oz) shredded coconut

50 g (1¾ oz) brown sugar

100 g (3½ oz) unsalted butter, melted

225 g (8 oz) cream cheese, softened

3 cups whipped cream, from a can

125 g (4½ oz) pure icing (confectioners') sugar

50 g (1¾ oz) white chocolate, melted

1 kg (2¼ lb) tinned peach slices

500 g (18 oz) peach jam

Grease a 12 cm (6 in) springform cake tin.

In a mixing bowl, add the biscuits, coconut and brown sugar and mix coarsely with a fork. Add the melted butter and mix together. Press evenly into the base of cake tin, then place in the fridge to chill.

In a large bowl, mix the cream cheese and whipped cream until combined. Add the icing sugar and mix again. Stir in the chocolate until you have a smooth and creamy mixture. Dice 75g (2½ oz) of the peach slices, and stir into the mixture.

Remove the tin from the fridge and pour in the cheesecake mixture. Cover loosely and return to the fridge for at least 2 hours, ideally overnight.

Before serving, heat a small saucepan over medium heat, add the jam and a tablespoon of water and stir until the jam dissolves into thick syrup. Leave to cool.

To serve, top the cheesecake with the remaining peach slices and pour over the cooled peach syrup.

3

SHORT *and* BOOZY

Born in Sicily and raised in New York City, Sophia Petrillo never minces words or cares for wasted time. So, it makes sense that her favourite drinks usually get straight to the point.

A classy and *suave cocktail*, but with a playful side – as indicated clearly by the pineapple wedge.

PINEAPPLE NEGRONI

SERVES 1

30 ml (1 fl oz) pineapple rum
30 ml (1 fl oz) Campari
30 ml (1 fl oz) sweet vermouth
pineapple wedge, for garnish

Combine the ingredients (except the garnish) in an old fashioned glass filled with ice. Stir.

Garnish with a pineapple wedge.

TROPICAL TEQUILA POTION

SERVES 1

4 slices cucumber, plus extra for garnish

45 ml (1½ fl oz) silver tequila

3 teaspoons Aperol

30 ml (1 fl oz) freshly squeezed lime juice

20 ml (¾ fl oz) sugar syrup

Muddle the cucumber slices (except the garnish) in a cocktail shaker. Add the other ingredients and fill the shaker with ice.

Shake vigorously.

Strain into an old fashioned glass and add a large ice cube. Garnish with a cucumber slice.

They say that *tequila* is the window to the soul. Or something like that. There are windows involved, for sure.

SHARK'S TOOTH

Make sure the rum here is *top-notch*, because you're certainly going to be able to taste it.

SERVES 1

- 30 ml (1 fl oz) good-quality aged rum
- 30 ml (1 fl oz) gold rum
- 3 teaspoons freshly squeezed lime juice
- 3 teaspoons pineapple juice, fresh if possible
- 3 teaspoons sugar syrup
- 1 teaspoon maraschino cherry liqueur (or juice)
- maraschino cherry, for garnish

Pour the aged rum into a shot glass or tumbler.

Place the remaining ingredients (except the garnish) in a high-speed blender with ½ cup crushed ice. Blend at high speed for 5 seconds.

Strain into a cocktail glass filled with crushed ice. Garnish with a maraschino cherry and serve with the aged rum on the side.

BLUE HAWAIIAN

SERVES 1

30 ml (1 fl oz) white rum

30 ml (1 fl oz) vodka

3 teaspoons blue curaçao

90 ml (3 fl oz) pineapple juice, fresh if possible

30 ml (1 fl oz) freshly squeezed lime juice

3 teaspoons sugar syrup

pineapple wedge and maraschino cherry, for garnish

Combine the ingredients (except the garnish) in a cocktail shaker filled with ice. Shake.

Strain into a tall glass filled with ice and garnish with a pineapple wedge and maraschino cherry.

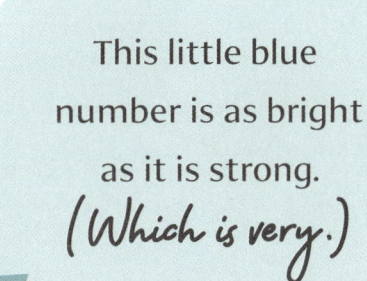

This little blue number is as bright as it is strong. *(Which is very.)*

SHRUNKEN SKULL

Evidently, Sophia likes to feel the *boozy burn* in each of her cocktails. This is no exception.

SERVES 1

- 30 ml (1 fl oz) white rum
- 30 ml (1 fl oz) demerara rum
- 30 ml (1 fl oz) grenadine
- 30 ml (1 fl oz) freshly squeezed lime juice
- pomegranate seeds, for garnish

Combine the ingredients (except the garnish) in a cocktail shaker filled with ice. Shake.

Strain into a skull-shaped tiki mug or old fashioned glass filled with ice.

Garnish with pomegranate seeds.

COBRA'S FANG

SERVES 1

3 teaspoons dark rum

30 ml (1 fl oz) 151 proof rum

2 teaspoons Pernod or absinthe

3 teaspoons freshly squeezed lime juice

3 teaspoons freshly squeezed orange juice

3 teaspoons Velvet falernum (page 146)

3 teaspoons grenadine

1 dash orange bitters

cinnamon stick, for garnish

Place the ingredients (except the garnish) in a high-speed blender with ½ cup crushed ice. Blend at high speed for 5 seconds.

Pour into an old fashioned glass and top with crushed ice. Garnish with a cinnamon stick.

This drink is a lot more enticing than its name might suggest. It goes without saying that it has plenty of *bite*.

Sophia's own *version* of the classic Nui Nui cocktail, but with a *heartier kick* of gold rum.

POINT *of* NUI RETURN

SERVES 1

60 ml (2 fl oz/¼ cup) gold rum

3 teaspoons freshly squeezed lime juice

3 teaspoons freshly squeezed orange juice

1½ teaspoons Cinnamon syrup (page 147)

1 teaspoon Allspice dram (page 145)

1 teaspoon Vanilla syrup (page 148)

1 dash orange bitters

pineapple wedge, lime wheel and mint sprig, for garnish

Place the ingredients (except the garnish) in a high-speed blender with 1 cup crushed ice. Blend at high speed for 5 seconds.

Pour into an old fashioned glass and top with crushed ice. Garnish with a pineapple wedge, lime wheel and fresh mint.

BARREL of RUM

SERVES 1

60 ml (2 fl oz/¼ cup) white rum

60 ml (2 fl oz/¼ cup) dark rum

60 ml (2 fl oz/¼ cup) freshly squeezed lime juice

60 ml (2 fl oz/¼ cup) freshly squeezed orange juice

60 ml (2 fl oz/¼ cup) freshly squeezed grapefruit juice

60 ml (2 fl oz/¼ cup) Passionfruit syrup (page 147)

1 teaspoon Honey syrup (page 148)

3 teaspoons soda water (seltzer)

1 teaspoon orange bitters

½ passionfruit

Place the white and dark rum, fruit juices, syrups, soda water and bitters in a high-speed blender with 1 cup crushed ice. Blend at high speed for 5 seconds.

Pour into a ceramic rum barrel mug or large brandy balloon. Top with the passionfruit half.

The name might sound straightforward, but this barrel holds a *delicate balance* of freshly squeezed fruit and, well, rum.

In *morse code*, the name of this cocktail makes the **letter V** to celebrate victory in war. A damn good occasion for a drink.

THREE DOTS *and* A DASH

SERVES 1

1 pineapple stick

3 maraschino cherries

30 ml (1 fl oz) rhum agricole (sugar cane rum)

30 ml (1 fl oz) aged rum

30 ml (1 fl oz) lime juice

3 teaspoons orange curaçao

3 teaspoons Honey syrup (page 148)

3 teaspoons Velvet falernum (page 146)

1½ teaspoons Allspice dram (page 145)

3 dashes orange bitters

To make the garnish, thread the pineapple stick and three cherries onto a skewer.

Place the ingredients (except the garnish) in a high-speed blender with ½ cup crushed ice. Blend at high speed for 5 seconds.

Pour into a short glass and top with crushed ice. Place the skewer across the top, ensuring that it's facing the right way so it reads as three dots and a dash.

GLASS SLIPPER

SERVES 1

60 ml (2 fl oz/¼ cup) rhum agricole (sugar cane rum)

20 ml (¾ fl oz) elderflower liqueur

20 ml (¾ fl oz) freshly squeezed lemon juice

3 teaspoons Vanilla syrup (page 148)

2 teaspoons 151 proof rum

edible flowers, for garnish

Combine the rhum agricole, elderflower liqueur, lemon juice and vanilla syrup in a cocktail shaker filled with ice. Shake.

Strain into an old fashioned glass filled with crushed ice. Float the 151 proof rum on top by pouring it over the back of a spoon. Garnish with edible flowers.

Some of us find our prince charming, and some of us just find a new cocktail. We know which Sophia would rather have.

POTTED PARROT

This nutty cocktail will have you flying around the bar *all night long*.

SERVES 1

60 ml (2 fl oz/¼ cup) white rum

3 teaspoons orange curaçao

60 ml (2 fl oz/¼ cup) freshly squeezed orange juice

30 ml (1 fl oz) freshly squeezed lemon juice

2 teaspoons Orgeat syrup (page 149)

2 teaspoons sugar syrup

mint sprig, for garnish

Combine the ingredients (except the garnish) in a cocktail shaker filled with ice. Shake.

Strain into an old fashioned glass filled with ice. Garnish with mint.

CRADLE of LIFE

SERVES 1

30 ml (1 fl oz) aged rum

30 ml (1 fl oz) spiced rum

3 teaspoons freshly squeezed lemon juice

3 teaspoons freshly squeezed lime juice (reserve 1 squeezed lime half for garnish)

3 teaspoons freshly squeezed orange juice

3 teaspoons Orgeat syrup (page 149)

½ teaspoon orange bitters

2 teaspoons green chartreuse

Combine the rums, fruit juices, syrup and bitters in a cocktail shaker (no ice). Shake.

Strain into an old fashioned glass filled with crushed ice.

Place the reserved lime half in the top of the drink.

Fill the lime cup with green chartreuse and carefully ignite. After 15 seconds, blow out the flame and tip the chartreuse into the drink.

This cocktail is *literally on fire*. A flaming lime looks cool (obviously) but please be sure to blow out the flame before taking a sip. *Please*.

Name a more iconic duo for a *tropical cocktail*. We'll wait.

RUM 'n' RASPBERRY

SERVES 1

60 g (2 oz/½ cup) fresh raspberries, plus extra for garnish

45 ml (1½ fl oz) spiced rum

3 teaspoons raspberry liqueur

3 teaspoons freshly squeezed lime juice

2 teaspoons agave syrup

1 dash orange bitters

Muddle the raspberries in a cocktail shaker. Add the remaining ingredients (except the garnish) along with ½ cup ice. Shake vigorously.

Strain the contents of the shaker into an old fashioned glass and top with ice if necessary. Garnish with extra raspberries.

HUKILAU

Like many tropical cocktails, the *hukilau* is as fun to say as it is to drink.

SERVES 1

- 30 ml (1 fl oz) spiced rum
- 3 teaspoons ginger liqueur
- 2 teaspoons amaretto
- 60 ml (2 fl oz/¼ cup) pineapple juice, fresh if possible
- 30 ml (1 fl oz) freshly squeezed orange juice
- 3 teaspoons freshly squeezed lime juice
- orange wheel and lime wedge, for garnish

Combine the ingredients (except the garnish) in a cocktail shaker filled with ice. Shake.

Strain into an old fashioned glass filled with ice. Garnish with an orange wheel and a lime wedge.

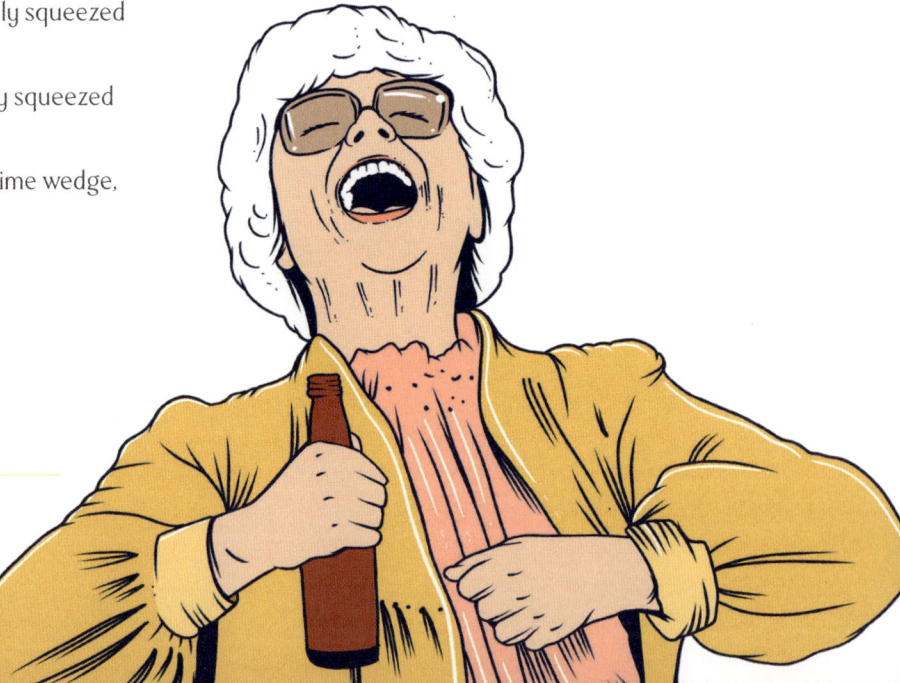

BEACHSIDE MANHATTAN

SERVES 1

30 ml (1 fl oz) aged rum

30 ml (1 fl oz) white rum

3 teaspoons sweet vermouth

3 teaspoons dry vermouth

1 dash orange bitters

orange slice and maraschino cherry, for garnish

Combine the ingredients (except the garnish) in a cocktail shaker filled with ice and stir vigorously.

Strain into a chilled cocktail glass. Garnish with an orange slice and a maraschino cherry.

As you might expect, this strong cocktail is a *beach chic* reimagining of the classic Manhattan.

El PRESIDENTE

SERVES 1

45 ml (1½ fl oz) white rum

45 ml (1½ fl oz) dry vermouth

1 teaspoon orange curaçao

½ teaspoon grenadine

orange twist and maraschino cherry, for garnish

Pour the ingredients (except the garnish) into a cocktail shaker filled with ice and stir vigorously.

Strain into a chilled cocktail glass.

Squeeze the orange twist over the drink to release the oils from the skin. Rub the rind along the rim of the glass. Drop the twist into the glass along with a maraschino cherry.

> In another life, Sophia could've been a *fearless dictator*. Or at the very least, a formidable but democratically elected leader.

TORTUGA

After one of these you'll feel like you're on a *Haitian vacation*. Or like you need an aspirin.

SERVES 1

45 ml (1½ fl oz) 151 proof rum

30 ml (1 fl oz) sweet vermouth

2 teaspoons orange curaçao

45 ml (1½ fl oz) freshly squeezed orange juice

3 teaspoons freshly squeezed lime juice

30 ml (1 fl oz) freshly squeezed lemon juice

2 teaspoons grenadine

mint sprig and orange wheel, for garnish

Place the ingredients (except the garnish) in a high-speed blender filled with ice. Blend at high speed until smooth.

Pour into a double old fashioned glass and garnish with mint and an orange wheel.

PAIN-KILLER

This cocktail was created by Pusser's Rum, and is based on a blended rum from an original Navy recipe. So you know it's *good*.

SERVES 1

60–90 ml (2–3 fl oz) aged rum

125 ml (4 fl oz/½ cup) pineapple juice, fresh if possible

30 ml (1 fl oz) freshly squeezed orange juice

3 teaspoons coconut cream

3 teaspoons sugar syrup

pineapple wedge, maraschino cherry and freshly grated nutmeg, for garnish

Combine the ingredients (except the garnish) in a cocktail shaker filled with ice. Shake.

Strain into an old fashioned glass filled with crushed ice. Garnish with a pineapple wedge, maraschino cherry and freshly grated nutmeg.

The HAGGARD MARINER

SERVES 1

30 ml (1 fl oz) demerara rum

30 ml (1 fl oz) dark rum

20 ml (¾ fl oz) freshly squeezed lime juice

3 teaspoons freshly squeezed grapefruit juice

3 teaspoons sugar syrup

1½ teaspoons Allspice dram (page 145)

mint sprig and lime wedge, for garnish

Combine the ingredients (except the garnish) in a cocktail shaker filled with ice. Shake.

Pour the contents of the shaker into a tiki mug or old fashioned glass and top up with more ice if necessary.

Garnish with mint and a lime wedge.

Based on the classic Ancient Mariner cocktail, this drink is named in honour of *how old* one feels after finishing it.

1988 MAI TAI

SERVES 1

45 ml (1½ fl oz) rhum agricole (cane juice rum)

30 ml (1 fl oz) demerara rum

30 ml (1 fl oz) dark spiced rum

3 teaspoons orange curaçao

3 teaspoons freshly squeezed lime juice

3 teaspoons Orgeat syrup (page 149)

3 teaspoons Velvet falernum (page 146)

pineapple wedge and maraschino cherry, for garnish

Combine the ingredients (except the garnish) in a cocktail shaker with ice. Shake.

Strain into an old fashioned or hurricane glass filled with crushed ice. Garnish with a pineapple wedge and a maraschino cherry.

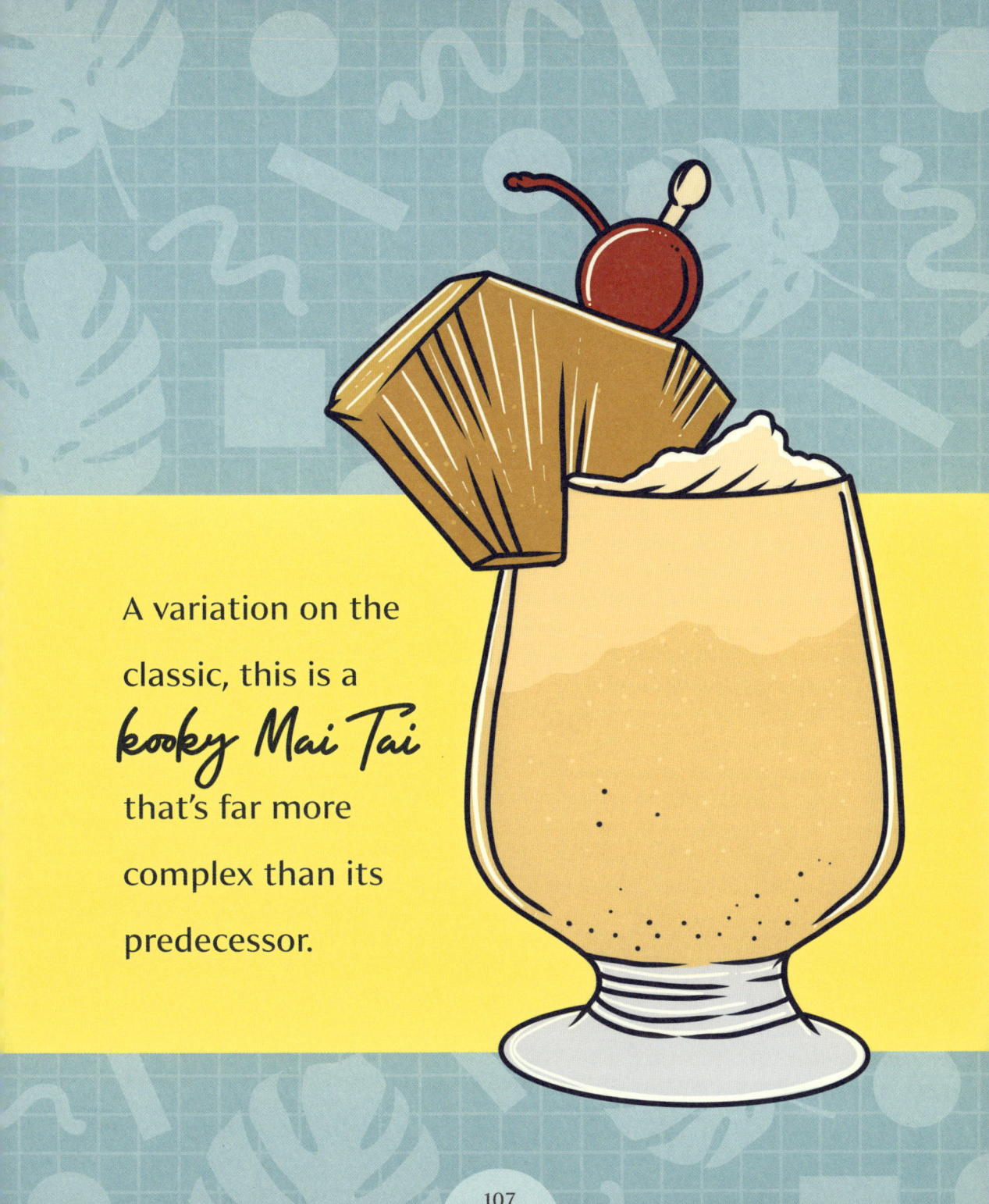

A variation on the classic, this is a *kooky Mai Tai* that's far more complex than its predecessor.

From our favourite Sicilian comes this traditional ricotta cheesecake recipe. *Bellissimo!*

SERVES 8

225 g (8 oz) self-raising flour

40 g (1½ oz) cornflour (corn starch)

100 g (3½ oz) caster (superfine) sugar

100 g (3½ oz) butter, softened

2 large eggs

1 tablespoon milk

400 g (14 oz) fresh ricotta, crumbled

225 g (8 oz) cream cheese, softened

2 teaspoons natural vanilla extract

25 g (1 oz) pure icing (confectioners') sugar

½ teaspoon ground cinnamon

Preheat the oven to 160°C (320°F) and grease a 23 cm (9 in) springform cake tin.

Combine the flour, cornflour, 40 g (1½ oz) of the caster sugar and butter in a food processor. When the mixture resembles breadcrumbs, add one egg and milk. Process until the mixture just comes together. Remove one third of dough and place in the fridge to chill.

Roll out the remaining dough until 5 mm (¼ in) thick. Gently place in the cake tin, and press into the base.

Beat the ricotta, cream cheese, remaining caster sugar and vanilla extract until smooth. Add the remaining egg and mix until combined. Spoon the mixture into cake tin.

Remove the dough from the fridge and roll out to the same thickness. Gently place on top of the cake tin, sealing the cheesecake. Press the edges together.

Bake for 50 minutes or until golden. Remove and cool, then chill overnight. To serve, dust the cheesecake with icing sugar and cinnamon.

4

DRINKING *all* DAY

Sweet, sweet Rose. A seasoned day drinker, she knows to play the long game with low-alcohol options, and a cheeky mocktail when needed.

Rose's personal variation on the Moscow Mule, this is a *summery* drink to sip all afternoon.

MIAMI MULE

SERVES 1

1 lime, cut into 8 pieces

1 small handful mint leaves

2 teaspoons sugar syrup

60 ml (2 fl oz/¼ cup) spiced rum

100 ml (3½ fl oz) ginger beer

mint sprig and lime wedge, for garnish

Muddle the lime and mint in a cocktail shaker. Add the sugar syrup, rum and 1 cup ice. Shake vigorously.

Pour the contents of the shaker into a copper mug or tall glass and add more ice if needed. Top up with ginger beer.

Garnish with fresh mint and a lime wedge.

HOME-OWNER'S MOJITO

SERVES 1

1 lime, cut into 12 pieces

155 g (5½ oz/1 cup) fresh blueberries, plus extra for garnish

1 small handful mint leaves

45 ml (1½ fl oz) white rum

30 ml (1 fl oz) umeshu (Japanese plum wine)

30 ml (1 fl oz) sugar syrup

60 ml (2 fl oz/¼ cup) soda water (seltzer)

lime wheel, for garnish

Muddle the lime, blueberries and mint in a cocktail shaker. Add the rum, umeshu and sugar syrup. Fill the shaker with ice and shake vigorously.

Pour the contents of the shaker into a tall glass and top up with ice.

Add the soda water. Garnish with extra blueberries and a lime wheel.

Blueberries are nature's *gift* to humankind, but they're damn expensive. So you probably own property if you're spending that blueberry money.

A great option if you'd like to feel like you just worked out, without ever leaving the comfort of the lanai.

SMOOTH SMOOTHIE

SERVES 1

30 ml (1 fl oz) aged rum

45 ml (1½ fl oz) cream liqueur

3 teaspoons oloroso sherry

¼ banana

3 teaspoons sugar syrup

pinch of salt

vanilla bean, for garnish

Place the ingredients (except the garnish) in a high-speed blender with 1 cup crushed ice. Blend at high speed for 5 seconds.

Pour into a milk bottle glass or highball glass. Garnish with a vanilla bean and drink through a straw.

SINGAPORE SLING

SERVES 1

30 ml (1 fl oz) gin

30 ml (1 fl oz) cherry brandy

30 ml (1 fl oz) orange curaçao

30 ml (1 fl oz) freshly squeezed lime juice

60 ml (2 fl oz/¼ cup) soda water (seltzer)

2 dashes orange bitters

maraschino cherry, for garnish

Pour the gin, cherry brandy, curaçao and lime juice into a tall glass filled with ice cubes. Top with the soda water.

Add the bitters and garnish with a maraschino cherry.

Created in Singapore's legendary *Long Bar*, this cocktail is an undisputed classic.

VIRGIN CAIPIRINHA

This alcohol-free version of the Brazilian classic has, on occasion, kept Rose doing the *Samba* till daybreak.

SERVES 1

1 lime, cut into 12 pieces

1 tablespoon soft brown sugar

60 ml (2 fl oz/¼ cup) ginger beer

lime wheel, for garnish

Muddle the lime and sugar in a cocktail shaker. Add the ginger beer and fill the shaker with ice.

Shake vigorously.

Pour the contents of the shaker into an old fashioned glass and garnish with a lime wheel.

GOLDEN COLADA

SERVES 1

45 ml (1½ fl oz) dark rum

30 ml (1 fl oz) gold rum

2 teaspoons Galliano

3 teaspoons coconut cream

40 ml (1¼ fl oz) freshly squeezed orange juice

30 ml (1 fl oz) pineapple juice, fresh if possible

pineapple wedge, for garnish

Place the ingredients (except the garnish) in a high-speed blender with 1 cup ice and blend at high speed until smooth.

Pour into a poco grande glass and garnish with a pineapple wedge.

Another member of the colada family, but nuanced with the legendary herbal liqueur *Galliano*.

COCONUT KISS

You can imagine Rose drinking a cocktail with the word *kiss* in it, right?

SERVES 1

- 30 ml (1 fl oz) coconut rum
- 30 ml (1 fl oz) white rum
- 20 ml (¾ fl oz) cherry brandy
- 30 ml (1 fl oz) cream
- 2 teaspoons grenadine
- maraschino cherry and grated coconut, for garnish

Combine the ingredients (except the garnish) in a cocktail shaker filled with ice. Shake.

Strain into a chilled cocktail glass and garnish with a maraschino cherry and grated coconut.

COCONUT RUM

SERVES 1

30 ml (1 fl oz) white rum

30 ml (1 fl oz) dark rum

3 teaspoons coconut rum

30 ml (1 fl oz) freshly squeezed lime juice

1 handful mint leaves, chopped

60 ml (2 fl oz/¼ cup) coconut water

3 teaspoons Orgeat syrup (page 149)

3 teaspoons sugar syrup

opened coconut, for serving (optional)

90 ml (3 fl oz) ginger beer

Combine the rums, lime juice, mint, coconut water and syrups in a cocktail shaker filled with ice. Shake.

Strain into a coconut (or a large cocktail glass) filled with crushed ice and top with the ginger beer. Drink through a straw.

It cannot be overstated how endlessly entertaining it is to drink out of *a coconut*.

Caffeine and alcohol are *yin and yang*, they are two sides of the same coin. Above all, they're delicious together.

BOOZY ICED COFFEE

SERVES 1

30 ml (1 fl oz) Jamaican rum

30 ml (1 fl oz) white rum

3 teaspoons coffee liqueur

20 ml (¾ fl oz) sweetened condensed milk

90 ml (3 fl oz) espresso, chilled

coffee beans, for garnish

Combine the ingredients (except the garnish) in a cocktail shaker filled with ice. Shake.

Strain into a tall glass filled with ice. Garnish with coffee beans.

'I'm not one to blow my own *vetugenfluke!*'

OUT *of* OFFICE

SERVES 1

30 ml (1 fl oz) white rum

3 teaspoons mango liqueur

3 teaspoons melon liqueur

3 teaspoons banana liqueur

60 ml (2 fl oz/¼ cup) freshly squeezed pink grapefruit juice

60 ml (2 fl oz/¼ cup) soda water (seltzer)

3 teaspoons cranberry juice

pineapple leaf and banana slice, for garnish

Pour the rum, liqueurs and grapefruit juice into a tall glass. Stir to combine.

Fill the glass with ice and top with soda water and cranberry juice.

Garnish with pineapple leaf and banana slice.

This drink is retirement in a glass. Made all the more so by a *pink flamingo* swizzle stick, if you can find one.

Sophisticated and elegant, just like Rose. Just make sure the ice is completely crushed for maximum *refreshment.*

MINT JULEP

SERVES 1

4 mint leaves

3 teaspoons mint syrup

60 ml (2 fl oz/¼ cup) bourbon

mint sprigs, for garnish

Muddle the mint leaves in a short glass. Add the syrup and bourbon and stir to combine.

Fill the glass with crushed ice and garnish with fresh mint.

WHISKEY SOUR

SERVES 1

60 ml (2 fl oz/¼ cup) whiskey

40 ml (1¼ fl oz) freshly squeezed lemon juice

20 ml (¾ fl oz) sugar syrup

1 egg white

maraschino cherry, for garnish

Combine the ingredients (except the garnish) in a cocktail shaker filled with ice and shake vigorously.

Strain into an old fashioned glass filled with ice. Garnish with a maraschino cherry.

Egg white, in a cocktail? Whoever thought of this was probably pooling some last ditch ingredients from the pantry.

AMARETTO SOUR

The almond liqueur in this sour cocktail brings with it a brilliant *nuttiness*.

SERVES 1

60 ml (2 fl oz/¼ cup) amaretto

40 ml (1¼ fl oz) freshly squeezed lemon juice

20 ml (¾ fl oz) Orgeat syrup (page 149)

1 egg white

maraschino cherry, for garnish

Combine the ingredients (except the garnish) in a cocktail shaker filled with ice and shake vigorously.

Strain into an old fashioned glass filled with ice.

Garnish with a maraschino cherry.

PIMM'S CUP

The most *British* of all mixed drinks, except perhaps a gin and tonic. But it's way more fun than that.

SERVES 1

30 ml (1 fl oz) gin

45 ml (1½ fl oz) Pimm's No 1

slices of cucumber, apple, orange, lemon and lime

6 mint leaves

90 ml (3 fl oz) ginger ale

Combine the ingredients in a tall glass filled with ice and stir.

SHIRLEY TEMPLE

SERVES 1

60 ml (2 fl oz/¼ cup) vodka

3 teaspoons freshly squeezed lime juice

90 ml (3 fl oz) ginger beer

3 teaspoons grenadine

1 tablespoon passionfruit pulp

orange wheel, for garnish

Pour the vodka and lime juice into a highball glass filled with ice and top with the ginger beer. Stir.

Slowly add the grenadine, pouring against the inside of the glass so that it sinks to the bottom.

Spoon the passionfruit pulp on top and garnish with an orange wheel.

Supposedly Shirley herself didn't like this cocktail at all, saying it was *far too sweet*. Rose would have to disagree.

GIN-EROL SPRITZER

SERVES 1

30 ml (1 fl oz) gin

30 ml (1 fl oz) Aperol

60 ml (2 fl oz) sparkling wine or soda water (seltzer)

orange wheel and green olives, for garnish

Combine the gin and Aperol in a large wine glass and fill with ice.

Top with sparkling wine or soda water, depending on how boozy you want to get.

Garnish with an orange wheel and olives.

Before *Aperol* became the trendiest summer cocktail, this classic gin version was always Rose's favourite day-drinking option.

MINT SPRIG MOCKTAIL

SERVES 1

60 ml (2 fl oz/¼ cup) cucumber juice

30 ml (1 fl oz) freshly squeezed lime juice

20 ml (¾ fl oz) grenadine

3 teaspoons sugar syrup

90 ml (3 fl oz) soda water (seltzer)

mint sprig and cucumber ribbon, to garnish

Combine the ingredients (except the garnish) in a tall glass filled with crushed ice and stir to combine.

Garnish with mint and a cucumber ribbon.

Refreshing and sans-booze, this minty drink is great if you need to go back to work after cocktail hour.

A close cousin of the piña colada but with a much *funnier name*. Arguably.

VIRGIN CHI CHI

SERVES 1

100 ml (3½ fl oz) pineapple juice, fresh if possible

20 ml (¾ fl oz) coconut cream

3 teaspoons sugar syrup

pineapple wedge and leaves, for garnish

Place the ingredients (except the garnish) in a high-speed blender with 1½ cups crushed ice. Blend until smooth.

Pour into a poco grande glass and garnish with a pineapple wedge and leaves.

BLOODY (ROSE) MARY

SERVES 1

45 ml (1½ fl oz) vodka

2 teaspoons dry sherry

2 teaspoons rich red wine

25 ml (¾ fl oz) freshly squeezed lemon juice

generous few dashes hot sauce

pinch of celery salt

freshly ground black pepper

90 ml (3 fl oz) good-quality tomato juice

pitted black olive, gherkin (pickle), barbecued prawn (shrimp), fried bacon strip and celery stalk, for garnish

Combine the vodka, sherry, wine, lemon juice, hot sauce, celery salt and pepper in a large glass. Stir. Fill with ice and top with the tomato juice.

Check the flavour and adjust to taste.

Thread an olive, gherkin and prawn onto a long skewer and place into the drink along with a strip of bacon and a celery stalk.

Hangover cure or high-altitude tipple – a Bloody Mary is a *vital cocktail*. This recipe includes Rose's favourite garnishes, but you can use whatever you like.

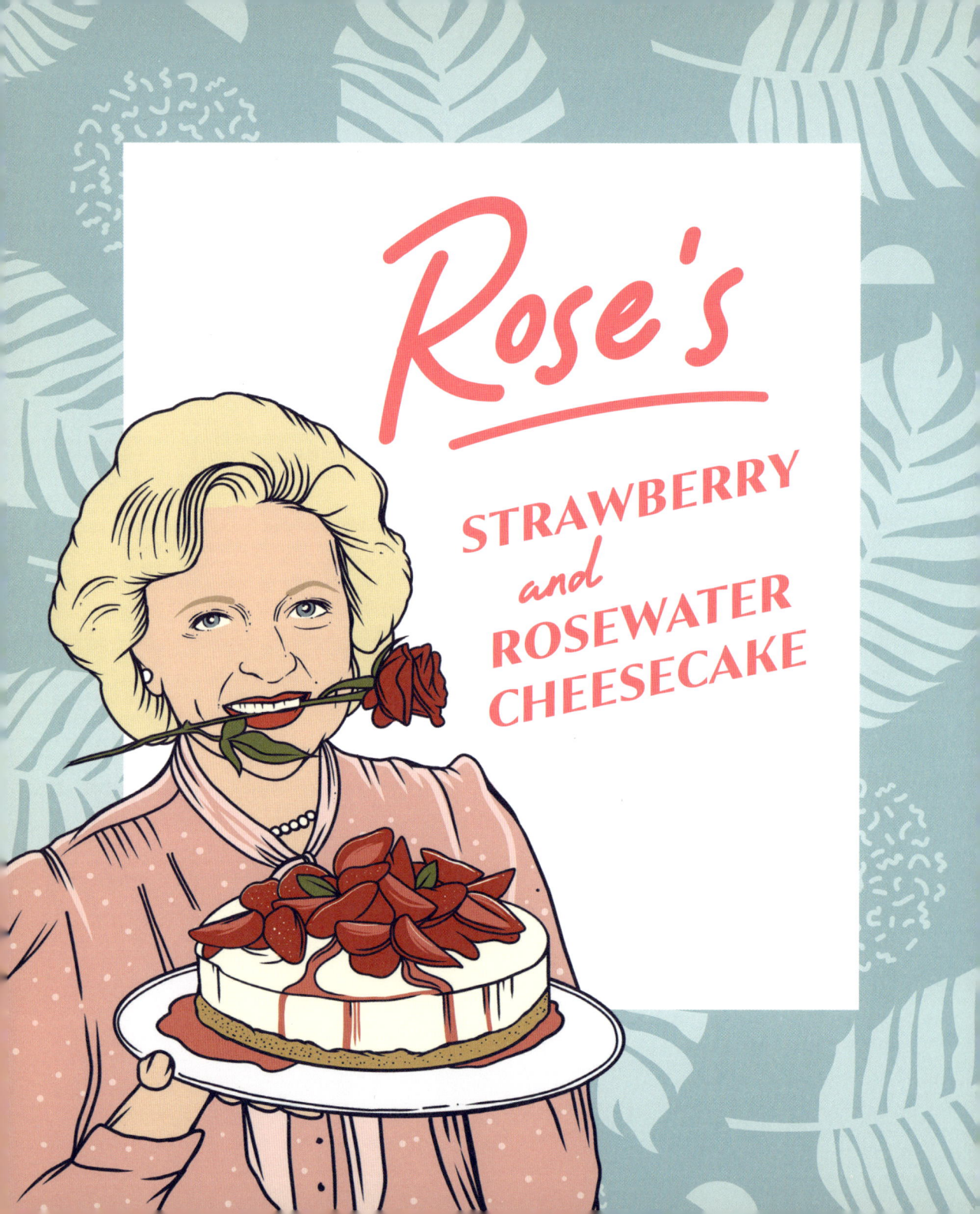

Afternoon tea, served with a sensible slice of cheesecake, is Rose's favourite time of day.

SERVES 8

250 g (8¾ oz) digestive biscuits (Graham crackers), crushed

100 g (3½ oz) unsalted butter, melted

4 gold-strength gelatine leaves

500 g (17½ oz) cream cheese

110 g (4 oz) caster (superfine) sugar

3 teaspoons rosewater

300 ml (10 fl oz) double (heavy) cream

160 g (5½ oz) rose petal or strawberry jam

250 g (8¾ oz) strawberries, sliced

Grease a 23 cm (9 in) springform cake tin.

Combine the crushed biscuits and butter, then press into the base of the cake tin.

Place the gelatine in a bowl of cold water, stand for 5 minutes, then drain and squeeze out the excess water. Return the gelatine to the bowl and pour over 60 ml (2 fl oz) boiling water. Whisk until dissolved, and then allow to cool slightly.

Blend the cream cheese and sugar in a food processor until smooth. Add the cooled gelatine and rosewater, and process to combine.

Using electric beaters, whip the cream until slightly thickened. Add the cream cheese mixture and beat until smooth, then pour over the crumb base. Cover loosely and chill for at least 2 hours, ideally overnight.

To serve, warm the jam in microwave for 30 seconds, then stir in the strawberries. Top the cheesecake with the strawberry mixture.

Basics

PEARL DIVER'S MIX

20 g (¾ oz) unsalted butter, softened

45 g (1½ oz) honey

1 teaspoon sugar syrup

½ teaspoon Cinnamon syrup (page 147)

½ teaspoon Vanilla syrup (page 148)

½ teaspoon Allspice dram (page 145)

Mix the ingredients together in a small bowl.

This pearl diver's mix will keep for 1 month in an airtight container in the fridge.

MAKES 4 PORTIONS

DON'S MIX

100 ml (3½ fl oz) Cinnamon syrup (page 147)

200 ml (7 fl oz) freshly squeezed grapefruit juice

Mix the ingredients together in a small bowl.

Don's mix will keep for 1 month in an airtight container in the fridge.

MAKES 300 ml (10 fl oz)

ALLSPICE DRAM

MAKES 750 ml (25½ fl oz/ 3 cups)

250 ml (8½ fl oz/1 cup) white rum

35 g (1¼ oz/¼ cup) allspice berries, lightly crushed

1 cinnamon stick

155 g (5½ oz) soft brown sugar

Combine the rum and allspice berries in a sterilised jar and seal. Store at room temperature for 5 days, shaking every day.

On day 5, break up the cinnamon stick and add to the jar. Steep for another 7 days, shaking every day.

Strain through a muslin cloth-lined sieve into a clean sterilised jar.

In a small saucepan over medium–high heat, combine the sugar with 375 ml (12½ fl oz/1½ cups) water. Stir until the sugar is dissolved, then set aside to cool.

Add the sugar syrup to the rum mixture and shake well to combine.

Leave the allspice dram to rest for at least 2 days before using. It will keep indefinitely.

VELVET FALERNUM

MAKES 750 ml (25½ fl oz/3 cups)

2 tablespoons blanched slivered almonds

40 cloves, crushed

185 ml (6 fl oz/¾ cup) white rum

zest of 9 limes

8 cm (3¼ in) piece fresh ginger, peeled and sliced

330 g (11½ oz/1½ cups) sugar

45 ml (1½ fl oz) freshly squeezed lime juice

¼ teaspoon almond extract

In a small dry frying pan over medium heat, toast the almonds and cloves until the almonds are golden. Transfer to a medium-sized sterilised jar, along with the rum, lime zest and ginger. Shake vigorously and leave to steep at room temperature for 24 hours.

Strain the rum mixture through a muslin cloth-lined sieve into a bowl. Squeeze the muslin to get all the oils out of the solids. Discard the solids.

In a clean sterilised jar, combine the sugar with 185 ml (6 fl oz/¾ cup) warm water and shake until the sugar is dissolved. Add the rum mixture, along with the lime juice and almond extract, and shake well to combine.

This velvet falernum will keep in the fridge for up to 1 month.

PASSIONFRUIT SYRUP

MAKES 100 ml (3½ fl oz)

pulp from 3 passionfruit

100 g (3½ oz) sugar

Place the passionfruit pulp and sugar in a small saucepan, add 100 ml (3½ fl oz) water and bring to the boil over medium–high heat. Stir until the sugar is dissolved. Set aside to infuse for at least 2 hours.

Strain into a sterilised bottle or jar. This passionfruit syrup will keep in the fridge for up to 1 month.

CINNAMON SYRUP

MAKES 250 ml (8½ fl oz/1 cup)

3 cinnamon sticks

220 g (8 oz) sugar

Lightly crush the cinnamon into pieces using a mortar and pestle. Transfer to a small saucepan, along with the sugar and 250 ml (8½ fl oz/1 cup) water. Bring to the boil over medium–high heat, stirring until the sugar is dissolved. Set aside to infuse for at least 2 hours.

Strain into a sterilised bottle or jar. This cinnamon syrup will keep in the fridge for up to 1 month.

VANILLA SYRUP

MAKES 500 ml (17 fl oz/ 2 cups)

1 vanilla bean, split open and seeds scraped

440 g (15½ oz/2 cups) sugar

1 teaspoon vanilla extract

Place the vanilla bean and seeds, sugar and 500 ml (17 fl oz/2 cups) water in a saucepan. Bring to the boil over medium–high heat and stir until the sugar is dissolved. Stir in the vanilla extract and set aside to cool.

Strain into a sterilised bottle or jar. This vanilla syrup will keep in the fridge for up to 1 month.

HONEY SYRUP

MAKES 500 ml (17 fl oz/ 2 cups)

350 g (12½ oz) honey

In a small saucepan over medium heat, combine the honey with 250 ml (8½ fl oz/1 cup) water. Gradually heat and stir until the honey is dissolved.

Pour into a sterilised bottle or jar. This honey syrup will keep in the fridge for up to 1 month.

ORGEAT SYRUP

MAKES 1 LITRE (34 fl oz)

500 g (1 lb 2 oz) raw almonds, soaked in warm water for 30 minutes

700 g (1 lb 9 oz) sugar

50 ml (1¾ fl oz) brandy

Drain the almonds and discard the water.

In a food processor, blend the almonds into a paste, adding a little water if needed. Transfer to a bowl and cover with 800 ml (27 fl oz) water. Leave to soak for 4 hours.

Strain the almond paste through a muslin cloth-lined sieve. Squeeze the cloth to extract the almond oils. Return the almond paste to the strained water and leave to soak for another 1–2 hours. Strain and squeeze again. Repeat the process once more if desired. Discard the almond paste.

In a medium-sized saucepan over low heat, gently bring the almond water to a simmer. Add the sugar and stir until dissolved. Remove from the heat and set aside to cool. Stir in the brandy.

Pour into a sterilised bottle or jar. This orgeat syrup will keep in the fridge for up to 3 months.

Drink index

151 Swizzle 58
1988 Mai Tai 106

A
Amaretto Sour 133
Apple Pie 36

B
Bahama Mama 17
Barrel of Rum 88
Beach-combing Bride ... 27
Beachside Manhattan ... 101
Bitter Mai Tai 33
Bloody (Rose) Mary 140
Blue Hawaiian 83
Blue Neon 39
Boozy Iced Coffee 125

C
Classic Daiquiri 48
Cobra's Fang 85
Coco Loco Pine-Lime .. 21
Coconut Kiss 121
Coconut Rum 122
Cradle of Life 96
Cuba Libre 32

D
Dark and Stormy 35

E
El Presidente 102

F
Federali 34
Frozen Lime Daiquiri ... 50
Frozen Marg 62

G
Gin-erol Spritzer 136
Glass Slipper 92
Golden Colada 120

H
Homeowners Mojito 114
Hukilau 100
Hurricane 16

J
Jet Pilot 64

L
Lit On Arrival 31

M
Mama's Pearls 55
Mango Daiquiri 51

Mara Amu 10
Miami Mule 113
Mint Julep 131
Mint Sprig Mocktail 135
Mojito 68
Montego Bay............. 67

O
Out of Office 128

P
Pain-killer................104
Passionfruit Marg 28
Pi Yi........................14
Pimm's Cup.............. 134
Piña Colada.............. 44
Pineapple Daiquiri........ 49
Pineapple Mojito 69
Pineapple Negroni 79

Point of Nui Return....... 87
Potted Parrot 93

Q
Queen's Park Swiz........ 61
Queen's Rd Cocktail 19

R
Rum Julep 66
Rum 'N' Raspberry....... 99
Rum Runner 13

S
Sailor on Leave........... 47
Salty Sailor 72
Shark's Tooth 82
Shirley Temple 135
Shrunken Skull........... 84
Singapore Sling 118

Smooth Smoothie....... 117
Stan's Mai Tai............ 22
Strawberry Daiquiri...... 52

T
Tangaroa.................. 18
Tequila Sunrise...........71
Test Pilot.................. 65
The Haggard Mariner .. 105
Three Dots and a Dash .. 91
Tortuga 103
Tropical Tequila Potion.. 80

V
Virgin Caipirinha.........119
Virgin Chi Chi...........139

W
Whiskey Sour...........132

Published in 2020 by Smith Street Books
Naarm | Melbourne | Australia
smithstreetbooks.com

ISBN: 978-1-925811-70-4

All rights reserved. No part of this book may be reproduced or transmitted by any person or entity, in any form or means, electronic or mechanical, including photocopying, recording, scanning or by any storage and retrieval system, without the prior written permission of the publishers and copyright holders.

Copyright text & design © Smith Street Books
Copyright illustrations © Mel Baxter

Publisher: Paul McNally
Project editor: Patrick Boyle
Designer: Kristy Lund-White
Design layout: Heather Menzies, Studio31 Graphics
Proofreader: Rachel Carter

Printed & bound in China by C&C Offset Printing Co., Ltd.

Book 131
10 9 8 7 6 5 4 3 2 1